This book belongs to

_____

This book is dedicated to my children - Mikey, Kobe, and Jojo.

Albert Einstein

By Mary Nhin

Pictures By
Yuliia Zolotova

College

$$R_1 = O2$$

$$2^2 =$$

$$V + k = O$$

$$a^\triangle ; t$$

$$E = mc^2$$

Some said I was a late bloomer. I didn't begin talking until later than my peers. When I did start, I hardly talked at all.

They didn't realize I was watching, observing, and thinking.

From the time I could remember, I loved math and science.

I was very curious about the world around me and how it worked.

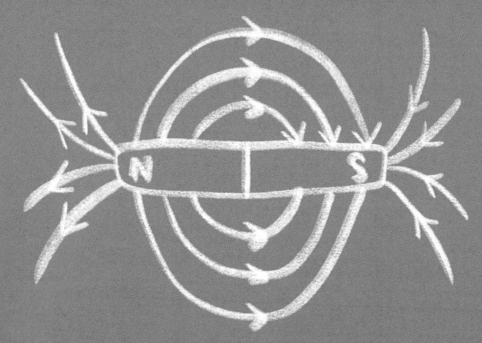

When I was introduced to a compass, I was fascinated by what was moving the needle. This was the beginning of my lifelong passion about invisible forces.

I was living in Germany at the time, and I was Jewish. Since Jews were discriminated against, that meant my education choices were limited. Even so, I didn't let that deter my natural curiosity for science and math.

I became acquainted with a tutor who introduced me to higher mathematics and philosophy. He gave me a geometry book which I devoured in very little time.

I taught myself algebra and Euclidean geometry over a single summer. I was only twelve years old!

In that same year, I discovered my own original proof of the Pythagorean theorem which is the relationship between the three sides of a right triangle. I wrote down my ideas and published my first research paper. In the scientific circle, to get a 'paper published' in a journal meant your work was being read by other scientists.

Soon, I went to college in Switzerland. I had dreams to teach. But after I graduated, I had a lot of trouble finding a teaching job.

Eventually, I landed a job in the patent office as an assistant examiner. There, I employed my scientific background to evaluate devices that were applying for patents. Even while working in the patent office, I didn't give up on my teaching and research dreams. I continued writing and developing my own scientific theories.

It was here in the patent office where I was able to see the physical effects of my theoretical concepts.

I would often be deep in thought. I even imagined riding a light beam. I developed a highly visual understanding of physics. Because of this unique thinking style, I filled my research papers with vivid, practical detail.

I employed thought experiments where I could show my concepts coming to life. A thought experiment is an experiment carried out in your imagination.

For special relativity, I employed moving trains and flashes of lightning to explain my insights.

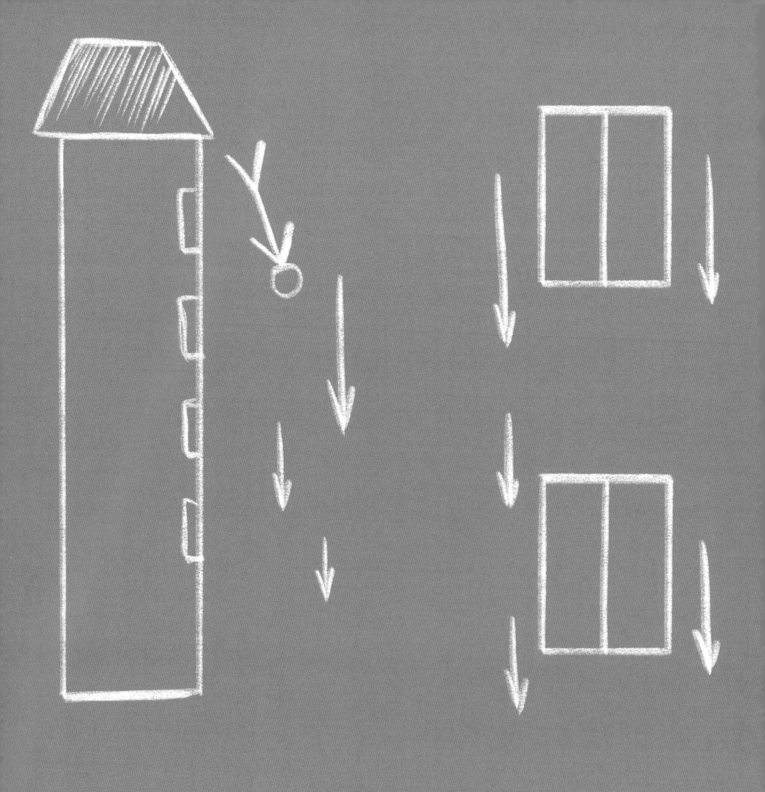

For general relativity, I considered a person falling off a roof, accelerating elevators, and blind beetles crawling on curved surfaces.

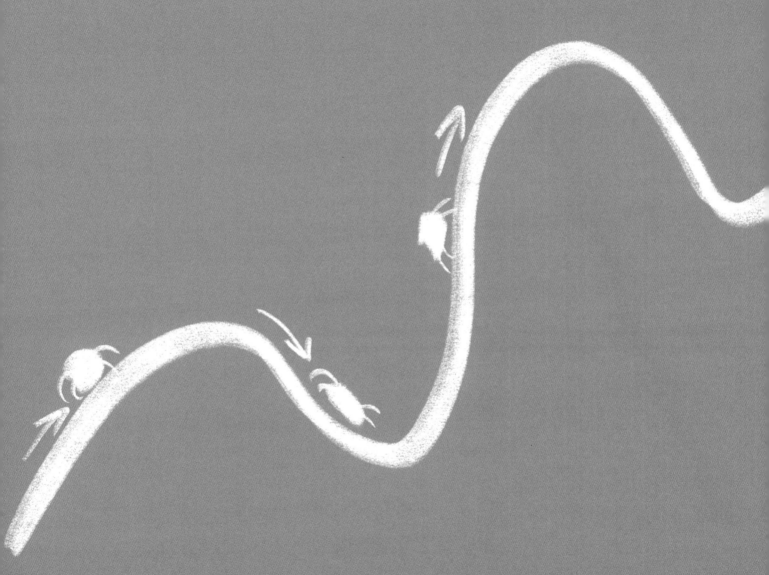

After many years of research, I published four revolutionary articles on photoelectric effect, Brownian motion, special relativity, and the equivalence of mass and energy. Many liked my work and thought it was groundbreaking. In fact, one of my theories, $E=MC^2$, became the most well known math equation in the world.

Soon after, I was asked to become a Professor of Theoretical Physics which I accepted. I was very happy. It meant I could carry on thinking and researching topics that were dear to my heart.

I was so surprised when I received a Nobel Prize for Physics for my explanation of the photoelectric effect.

The true sign of intelligence is not knowledge but imagination.

Timeline

1879 - Born in Germany

1900 - Graduates college

1902 - Starts job at Patent Office

1905 - Albert publishes four groundbreaking
papers on photoelectric effect, Brownian motion,
special relativity, and the equivalence of mass and energy

1922 – Albert is awarded the 1921 Nobel Prize in Physics

1940 - Albert becomes a U.S. citizen

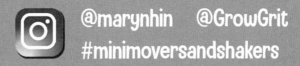

Made in the USA
Middletown, DE
15 September 2022

10587132R00022